# The POST OFFICE
## Project Book

### JEAN BARROW

**Note to the reader**

Both men and women work for the Post Office today, but in this book the people who sort and deliver the mail have all been called 'postmen'. It was decided that this would be easier to read than 'postmen and postwomen'.

Headway · Hodder & Stoughton

# Sending a letter before 1840

*Today, a letter written by any one of us can travel less than a mile or as far as we wish within the British Isles for the price of the same first or second-class stamp.*

Before 1840, letters were charged on the distance they had travelled from London and the number of sheets of paper used. Compared with today, the price of sending a letter was high.

Envelopes were not used, as these counted as an extra sheet of paper, and two sheets cost twice as much as one. Instead, letters were carefully folded, with the address written on one side and the other side sealed with wax.

People used large sheets of paper, or wrote in very tiny writing to avoid the extra cost of postage. They were even known to give the paper a half turn and to continue writing across what they had already written.

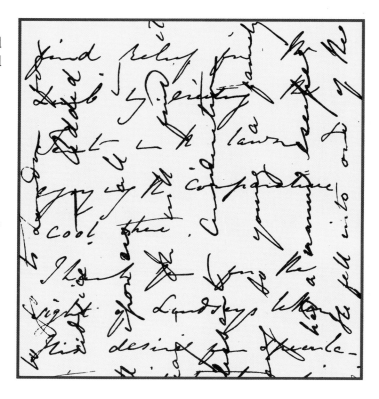

*Below, a letter sealed with wax, sent in the early part of the English Civil War (1642–1646) to Sir Ferdinando Fairfax, who commanded the Parliamentary army, urging him for help in York, which the king's army was then beseiging.*

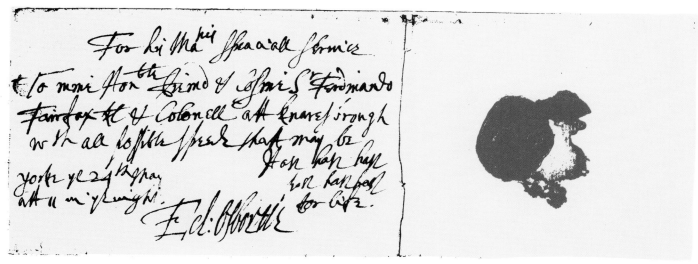

## Writing home

Before 1840, it was the person who received the letter who paid the postage and not the sender, so many poor people were unable to keep in touch with relations because they could not afford to pay the postage of letters addressed to them.

Some boarding-school boys used to use a special code on the outside of letters to let their parents know when they were due home for the holidays. When their letter was delivered by the Letter Carrier, a quick glance told their parents all they needed to know and they would refuse to pay for the letter.

Newspapers were sent free of charge, as long as no message had been written on them, so secret messages were often written using milk in place of ink. The paper then had to be heated to bring out the writing.

Another method was to prick holes, or to place a tiny dot, over the top of letters or words to spell out messages. A tiny hole or dot over one of the numbers in the date on the newspaper showed on which page the message appeared.

# Post Office reform

*A man called Rowland Hill argued that it should not cost any more to send a letter from London to Edinburgh than it did to send it locally.*

Initially, a number of people disagreed with Rowland Hill, but he was convinced that if the cost of sending a letter was cheaper, more people would write letters.

Rowland Hill also wanted letters to be paid for at the time of posting. He knew this would speed up delivery, as there would be no need to knock on doors. However, there was a great deal of opposition by the public to cutting a slit in their front door.

There was another delivery problem. Although house numbering started in 1767, many houses still had no numbers, and the people who did have them tried to take their number with them when they moved! The same street numbers could be found over and over again within short distances of each other. Also, many roads had the same name, with Victoria being one of the most popular.

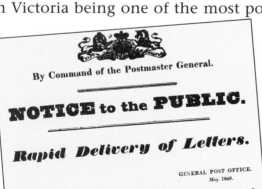

By Command of the Postmaster General.

## NOTICE to the PUBLIC.

### Rapid Delivery of Letters.

GENERAL POST OFFICE.
*May. 1849.*

The Postmaster General is desirous of calling attention to the greater rapidity of delivery which would obviously be consequent on the general adoption of **Street-door Letter Boxes, or Slits,** in private dwelling houses, and indeed wherever the Postman is at present kept waiting.

He hopes that householders will not object to the means by which, at a very moderate expense, they may secure so desirable an advantage to themselves, to their neighbours, and to the Public Service.

*Above, Rowland Hill (1795–1879),who established the modern postal system, and left, the poster issued in 1849 by the Postmaster General, urging people to cut letter boxes in their front doors.*

From 10 January 1840, all letters under ½ oz (10 g) in weight could be sent anywhere in the British Isles for just one penny.

Envelopes started to be used, but at this stage they were not gummed so people either had to gum them themselves or continue to use wax to seal their letters.

# Now you see

1 Write a letter to a friend, leaving a wider than normal space between the lines. Write another message in these spaces using an invisible ink which will appear when the paper is heated with a warm iron. For ink, try using lemon juice, onion juice or a teaspoon of salt, sugar or honey dissolved in a glass of water. Experiment with other items yourself, including fizzy drinks.

2 How small can you make your handwriting? Write a letter to a friend on a piece of paper 5 cm by 7 cm. Try writing a letter, then giving it a half turn before continuing further. How easy is it to read? When you have written your letter, fold it so that there are four overlapping corners. Seal it with a blob of sealing wax.

3 Carry out a survey of people's front doors. Look at style and colour. Where are the house numbers? Would they be visible from the front gate after dark? Some houses have names as well as numbers. Which house has the most unusual name? Where are the letter boxes? Will the postman or woman have to bend down to deliver the mail?

# Your mail

*Do you eagerly await the arrival of the postman or woman and the click of the letter box as the family's mail drops on to your mat?*

Are you one of those people who, on receiving a letter, quickly slits open the envelope in a rush to see what's inside? Or do you savour the moment, carefully fingering the envelope, glancing at the postmark and saying, 'who do I know in Cornwall?' or wherever, and,'Is that Grandma's spidery handwriting?'

An envelope can tell you lots of things. Did the sender want you to receive the letter quickly and therefore included your postcode and stuck a first-class stamp on to the top right-hand corner? Is your letter in a long brown envelope with a neatly typed name and address? Perhaps it's an important letter from school. Sometimes people receive a 'window envelope' – an envelope with a 'see through' plastic oblong window low down on the front. This often means it is a bill or a business letter. The name and address are printed on the paper inside instead of on the envelope. The paper is then carefully folded so it can show through the window.

## Postmarks and slogans

Along the top of an envelope and over the postage stamp a machine prints a red or black circular mark called a postmark. This will often be accompanied by an advertising catch-phrase or postmark slogan.

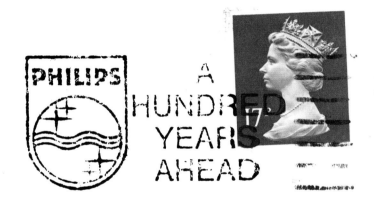

A postmark is used to cancel the stamp so that it cannot be used again. The postmark will tell you two or three things:

- the district and county where the letter was posted
- the date the letter was posted
- and sometimes the time the letter was collected by the postman.

One of the most used postmark slogans is 'Pass on your Postcode'. Slogans are changed fairly frequently by the Post Office; big organisations also use them to advertise an event or a charity, and firms use them to advertise themselves.

R.D Jones
32 High Street
Upton
Glos. GL7 1BB

# Now you see

1 Carry out a survey for up to one month of the different types of post arriving at your home – private, business, postcards, circulars, foreign, parcels, packets and so on – and then make a bar chart. Which member of your family receives the most post? Why do you think this is?

2 Make a note of the towns where the above letters were posted. Mark each town with a mapping pin on a large map of the British Isles. Locate your home town and use coloured thread to show the journeys taken by all your incoming mail.

3 Take various types and sizes of envelopes to pieces to see how they are made. Try making your own, including a 'window' envelope.

4 Make a collection of postal slogans and keep them either in a scrapbook or in plastic sleeves. If a friend is making a collection, keep duplicates for swaps.

# Out and about with the postman

*Have you ever wondered what it must be like to be out and about very early in the morning in all weathers?*

The postman on his walk, the milkman on his rounds and the paper boy or girl who delivers newspapers and magazines before going off to school, are all up and about very early.

The postman and the milkman keep a close eye on the elderly people living alone. They are perhaps the only ones the elderly folk will talk to that day. In very rural areas, postmen will do the odd bit of shopping for the elderly.

Do you know your postman? Or perhaps the question should be, do you know *all* your postmen? Most postmen work shifts in a four-man group, so you might see each one only at four-weekly intervals. Each area a postman delivers to is called a **walk**, regardless of how he travels.

How does your postman travel to your home? If you are in a town, your postman might walk with his pouch slung over his shoulder, or if you live in a busy town near to shops and offices which receive a great deal of mail, your postman might push the mail on a trolley.

*This postwoman is carrying her letters in a pouch.*

*This postman has a lot of mail to deliver, so he uses a trolley to do his walk.*

In rural areas, the postman travels in a van. If this is how you receive your mail, look for the Post Office number somewhere on the van. You will find that although you have different postmen, the van is always the same. That is because a van is assigned to a journey and not to a person.

In more isolated areas, there are postbuses. These carry passengers as well as mail, and operate where there is no public transport. The drivers are all postmen or postwomen. Scotland has more postbuses than anywhere else, with Wales coming second. If you have not seen any of these in your area, watch out for one when you are on holiday. You might even be able to ride in one.

Other methods of travel that today's postmen use are:

- four-wheel drive vehicles for rough areas
- bicycles in towns
- rowing boats which are used to row mail out to people on small islands and to ships in ports.

*Below, a postwoman on her bicycle, and below right, a rowing boat used by the Post Office to deliver mail to islands.*

BICYCLES WERE FIRST USED IN 1883 WHEN THE VOLUME OF MAIL INCREASED. ONE INVENTION WAS NICKNAMED THE 'HEN AND CHICKENS' BECAUSE THERE WAS ONE LARGE WHEEL (THE HEN) IN THE CENTRE AND FOUR SMALL ONES (CHICKENS) TO ACT AS A BALANCE.

# The postman's job

*A postman's job is not just a matter of delivering the mail. He reports for duty at the sorting office as early as five o'clock in the morning.*

Before going out to deliver his letters and small packets, the postman's first task is to sort the piles of local mail into areas and streets.

The postman then collects a sack, or **drop bag** as it is called, containing packets and large envelopes for his walk. These are too bulky for the machinery and have been sorted and cancelled by hand in another part of the sorting office.

The letters and packets are put into bundles held together with elastic bands. These bundles are put in order of delivery into the postman's pouch, or into a tray if the postman is travelling by van.

In areas where there is a great deal of mail, the postman will have more than one bag. He will only carry one pouch and will arrange for somewhere on his walk (usually a newsagents or post office) to be used as a pick-up point for the second bag.

The postman now goes to the **cage** (a small office behind a metal grille) to see if there is any registered or special delivery mail. These items are added to the pouch in a special pocket.

The postman's last job in the sorting office is to collect some sacks and his keys for emptying the post boxes. He also needs his vehicle key and log book if he is travelling by van.

Before going out on his round, the postman will take half an hour's break for breakfast as he gets up so early.

*Sorting the mail by hand into areas and streets to make delivery easier.*

10

*A postman's pouch.*

ONLY 30 PER CENT OF MAIL NOW TRAVELS BY RAIL. THE OTHER 70 PER CENT TRAVELS BY ROAD, OFTEN THROUGH THE NIGHT.

POSTMEN ALSO WORK AT AIRPORTS, HELPING TO SPEED THE THREE MILLION FIRST-CLASS LETTERS THAT ARE CARRIED BY AIR EVERY NIGHT.

THE POST OFFICE HANDLES OVER 30 MILLION LETTERS A DAY, FROM MONDAY TO FRIDAY.

# Now you see

If you happen to be going on a train journey one day, you might recognise your postman working on the railway platform sorting bags of mail into wire cages. Some will be destined for other parts of the country and will be waiting to be put aboard a train while other mail will have just arrived and will be about to be delivered to the local sorting office. Take a quick glance at the labels attached to the bags to see where they are going.

# Uniforms through the years

*What uniform does your postman wear, and does it change with the seasons? Every postman/woman is issued with:*

- a coat
- two pairs of trousers/slacks or two skirts
- a tie, belt and pullover
- four shirts/blouses
- a cold weather coat, and cap or beret
- two security badges
- a pair of snow chains.

New recruits are supplied with just an arm band.

*1793 London 'General Post' Letter Carrier – the name given to postmen before 1883. The blue waistcoat had brass buttons which showed the wearer's Post Office number.*

Look closely at the postman's security badge. It is bronze and Post Office red. The top third says 'Royal Mail', the middle bronze portion tells you the postman's number and the bottom red bit tells you the postal district in which your postman works.

Every postman has a chance of promotion which means working on registered mail or becoming a code operator. They will then be known as Postman/woman Higher Grade and their badge will be blue instead of red.

Uniforms have kept to three main colours over the years – red, blue and grey.

At first, the men of the Post Office were angry about having to wear a uniform. They thought the Post Office believed them to be dishonest and that the uniform was an easy way of being able to keep an eye on them. In 1837, the men delivering London's locally posted letters were given a similar beaver hat but a blue coat with a scarlet collar.

*The blue uniform of the Letter Carriers, issued in 1837.*

In 1984, the uniform reverted to navy blue with scarlet trim. Today, even the postman or woman's pouch is navy and scarlet as is his or her waterproof jacket.

In those days, Letter Carriers were given very grand coats and beaver hats but not issued with trousers! A number of cartoons appeared in newspapers making fun of these carriers of the post, showing them wearing a nightshirt under their uniform jacket.

In 1855 London's local Letter Carriers and the 'General Post' Letter Carriers were issued with grey trousers and a return to the scarlet jacket. However, the scarlet uniform was eventually discarded when it was realised how much it showed the dirt, and navy blue, today's colour, was chosen.

In 1969 the uniform colour again changed, this time to grey.

## Now you see

With your friends, design a uniform for the postman of the future. Send it to the Head Postmaster at your main post office and ask for his comments.

WHEN CHRISTMAS CARDS WERE FIRST SENT IN THIS COUNTRY, THE POSTMEN WORE SCARLET TUNICS AND WERE KNOWN AS 'ROBIN POSTMEN'. SO IT WASN'T LONG BEFORE THE ROBIN REDBREAST STARTED APPEARING ON THE GREETING CARDS!

# Postal Cadets

*Young people of 16 or 17 can join the Post Office as Postal Cadets, and take part in a varied and exciting programme.*

Postal Cadets work shift hours learning about the Post Office between 6 am and 10 pm. They are given the opportunity to develop personal skills such as computer operation, first aid, working in teams and learning to drive.

They also work in small groups on interesting and fun projects – such as looking at the collection and history of postage stamps with a trip to the Philatelic Bureau in Edinburgh and other countries. Projects do not necessarily have a link with the Royal Mail. The young Cadets carry out recycling projects, and community awareness is encouraged with sponsored events organised to support local charities.

Most Cadets have the opportunity of travelling abroad to do research into postal developments. A visit to Paris would involve looking at inward letters travelling from France to Britain, comparing each country's postal systems and maybe putting recommendations to the Royal Mail. Another time conservation and environmental work might be carried out in the EEC. Cadets are encouraged to come up with ideas for projects and if going abroad, are expected to make their own arrangements and to establish their own contacts in the chosen country.

## Becoming a Postal Cadet

After applying to become a Postal Cadet, the candidate is given a test where speed counts. One section is entitled 'Spot the Difference'. Try this example:

| Mr Brown | Mr Brown |
| 123 Lodge Road | 123 Lodge Road |
| BRIGHTON | BRIGHTON |
| Sussex BN9 6BA | Sussex BN6 9BA |

Around 100 addresses are listed with a time limit for completion.

If a young person does well at this test, he or she is given an interview and asked to fill in a form about themselves, for example:

- How good are you at getting up in the morning?
- If you have to start work at 6 am, how will you travel here?
- How do your parents feel about you wanting to become a Postal Cadet?

He or she is also asked simple geography questions such as 'Where are the Isle of Man, Truro, and the Isle of Skye'?

# Royal Mail Parcel Force

*Watch out for these bright red vans and lorries with their distinctive logo.*

Have you ever received a parcel that has had to be repacked by the Post Office? A large number of parcels never reach their destination because they have been badly packed or addressed.

Always remember to put your full address on the back of the parcel at right angles to the destination address so that, if need be, the parcel can be returned to you without having to be opened by the Post Office. Items should be wrapped in strong brown paper, then secured with adhesive tape and tied up with string.

TODAY, OVER 1 MILLION ITEMS ARE CARRIED EACH WORKING DAY TO DESTINATIONS AT HOME AND TO AROUND 200 COUNTRIES WORLDWIDE.

THE POST OFFICE INTRODUCED A PARCEL POST IN AUGUST 1883 AND THE COST WAS ONE OLD PENNY FOR UP TO 1 LB (454 G).

## Now you see

1 Learn to tie two knots – the reef knot and the surgeon's knot:

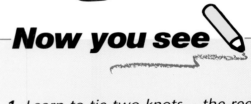

Surgeon's Knot

Reef Knot          Stage 1          Stage 2

The surgeon's knot is a very secure knot and is ideal for parcels.

2 Practise tying up a parcel. First try something easy such as a book and then something more difficult. Try a teddy bear which is soft and unbreakable, or a china mug which is easily broken. How can you protect certain items from being damaged while on their journey?

# Post office counters

*Do you visit your post office just to buy stamps or to post a parcel? Post offices do more than just accept mail and sell stamps; they are a very thriving business.*

In the picture above you can see some of the many things you can obtain through your post office: a passport, a TV licence, phonecards, a postal order, a European driving licence, a weekly pension book and a car tax disc.

In rural areas, it is not unusual to see post offices taking up part of a chemist, grocery or stationery shop. Sometimes they might even be found in one room of a small cottage.

*THE OLDEST POST OFFICE IN GREAT BRITAIN IS IN DUMFRIES.*

*ACCORDING TO THE GUINNESS BOOK OF RECORDS, THE POST OFFICE IN GEORGE SQUARE IN GLASGOW IS 47.8 M LONG AND HAS 27 POSITIONS.*

*THE UK HAS MORE THAN 21,000 POST OFFICE COUNTERS.*

# THE POST OFFICE GAME

| | |
|---|---|
| **Number of players:** | two |
| **Things you will need:** | a dice |
| | a pair of scissors |

## Preparation
Pull out the two centre pages. Cut out the keys and the two post vans. The rest forms the baseboard for the game.

## Aim
To be the first to complete the round and empty all four post-boxes.

## Rules
Each player chooses a van and a set of four keys. Place the vans in the sorting office. Throw the dice to see who starts.

Take it in turn to throw the dice and move from square to square. If you land on a coloured square, follow the instruction on it. If you land on a post-box, leave your key with the same number as the box on the square.

If you land on a post-box and the other player has already collected the mail and left their key, you cannot leave yours. You must wait for the next collecting time after you arrive back at the sorting office. Once there, still taking it in turn, you must throw any remaining key numbers to empty each post-box. Put your van on each box you have to visit to leave your key and jump straight on to the next box when you throw the right number, ignoring any squares with instructions.

Two vans are not allowed on post-box squares together. The second player to arrive must wait a turn and try again.

When you have got rid of all your keys, throw the dice and move round the board to get back to the sorting office. You must throw the exact number to get back into the sorting office at the end.

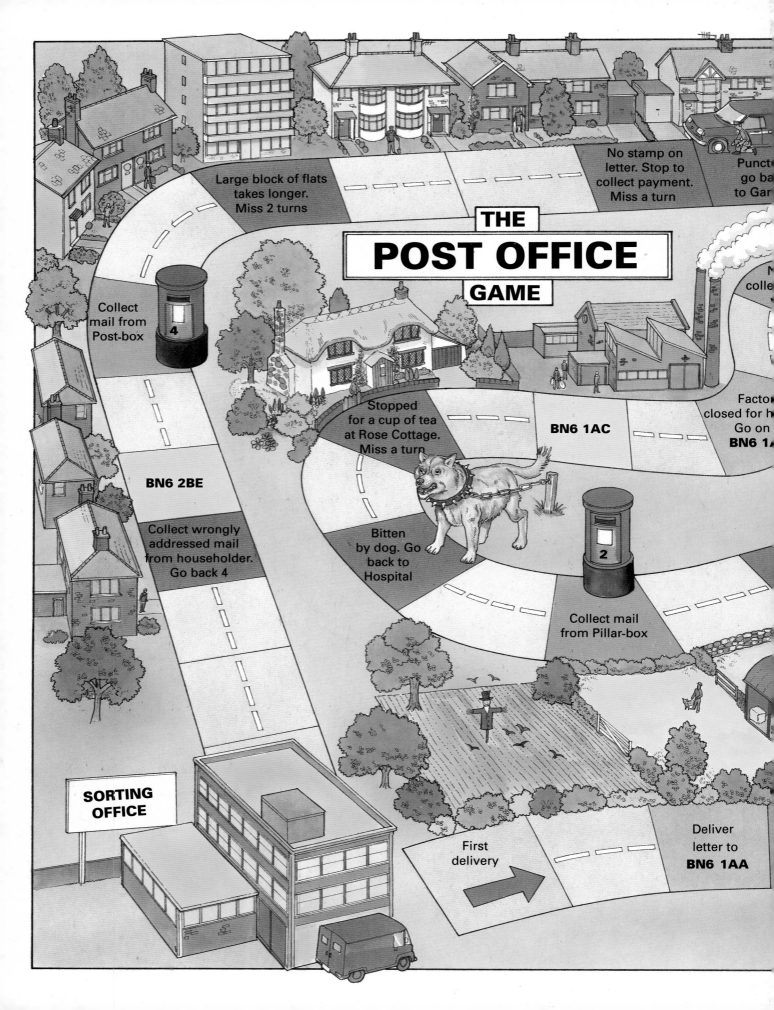

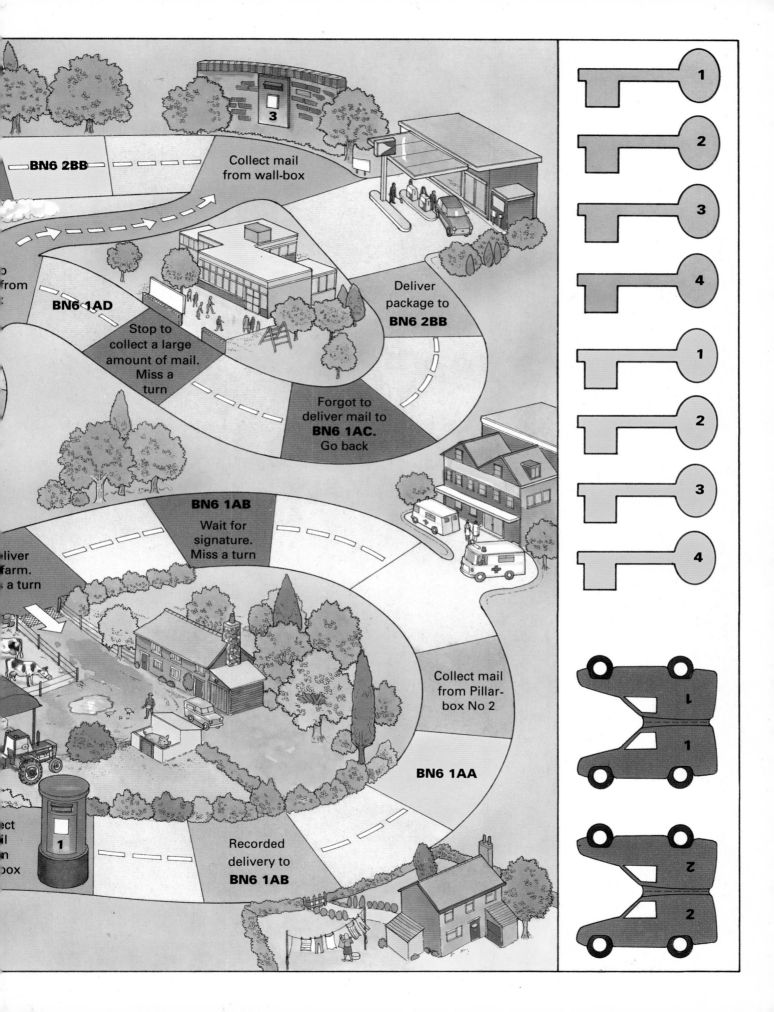

BN6 2BB

Collect mail from wall-box

3

from

BN6 1AD

Stop to collect a large amount of mail. Miss a turn

Deliver package to **BN6 2BB**

Forgot to deliver mail to **BN6 1AC**. Go back

**BN6 1AB**
Wait for signature. Miss a turn

liver farm. a turn

Collect mail from Pillar-box No 2

**BN6 1AA**

ect il n ox

Recorded delivery to **BN6 1AB**

1

2

3

4

1

2

3

4

1

1

2

2

The layout inside one post office is very much like another because they all have the same job to do. Each post office has a counter with one or more serving positions. Close by each one are scales for weighing letters, small packages and parcels for destinations around the British Isles and abroad.

People queue alongside a rail, and as a position becomes free the person in front goes forward to be served. This is considered a much fairer way of queuing. If there is a bit of a wait, there are now video displays advertising goods and local events to help while away the time.

Because post offices large and small provide such a variety of services, they have become meetings places for people within the local community.

## Now you see

1 How many positions are there in your main post office? Do they all do the same job? Try to discover ways in which your post office is trying to speed up the waiting times. Make out a plan of how the post office is arranged.

2 How do the collection times at the main post office compare with the posting boxes in the street? Is there just one collection box or several? If there are more than one, do they take different types of mail?

# Posting boxes

*Do you know where each post-box is situated in your area, or do you regard them as just another piece of street furniture and take them for granted? Post-boxes are, in fact, extremely interesting and it is well worth stopping to take a good look at them.*

Try to be around when the postman arrives to empty the post-box. The collection plate will tell you when he is due. He will take a mail bag from his van and unlock the post-box with a key from his bunch. Inside the box, the letters are held behind a strong wire grille so that when the door is opened the letters will not fall all over the ground.

The postman positions his mail bag at the bottom of the wire grille and releases a metal chute which guides the letters and small packages into his sack. When this is done, the postman alters the collection number at the top of the door before going on his way.

*THERE ARE AT LEAST 8 DIFFERENT MANUFACTURERS OF THE EIIR LAMP BOX.*

There are three types of post-boxes:

- pillar boxes which are usually found standing by the roadside
- wall boxes built into a wall
- lamp boxes fixed to posts.

Many of these come in all shapes and sizes with different markings. Boxes can be found from every region since Queen Victoria: Edward VII, George V, George VI and Elizabeth II. Look carefully at the crowns, which often differ from each other. Sometimes the name of the manufacturer who made the box also appears. Scotland has had its own design of post-boxes since 1954. They do not bear the royal cipher, EIIR, only the crown.

The Ludlow letter box was named after James Ludlow, its manufacturer. These boxes were made of wood and reinforced with steel. They were made especially for small post offices in country areas.

*This small Victorian Ludlow box, in Sevenoaks, Kent, is rather rare. Notice that it also has the initials GR on the plate.*

*THE FIRST POST-BOXES WERE GREEN, BUT PEOPLE THOUGHT THEY WERE TOO DIFFICULT TO FIND AS THEY BLENDED INTO THE SURROUNDINGS.*

# Now you see

Taking photographs or making drawings of post-boxes could become an absorbing hobby. Make a study of those in your area and also of any you can find when on holiday in this country or abroad. Which is the oldest box you can find? Remember that some boxes will be in walls. Do they vary in size and shape? Do they all have the same sized posting slot? Look out for the variety of initials and crowns. Make a collection of manufacturers' names.

# Postcodes

*Today, every one of the British Isles's 24 million addresses has a postcode and all of these addresses are on one computer disc, making a wonderful map reference of the whole country.*

A postcode is a simple form of address and is in two halves:

TN9 1AB

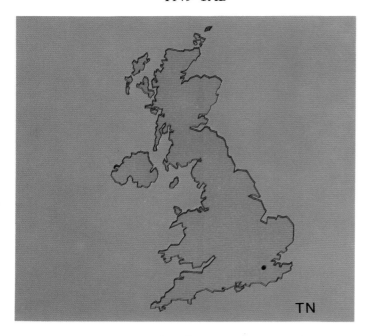

The first part is the postcode area, for example, 'TN' refers to 'Tonbridge' in this particular code.

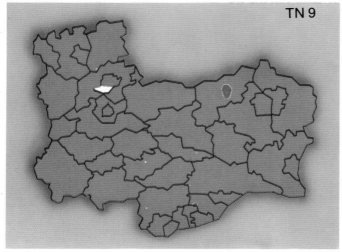

The TN area is divided into districts and it is this first part of the code that is used to send a letter to the office that will sort and deliver your letter. In this case, the letter will be sent to the office responsible for district 9.

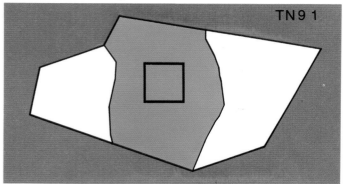

The second part of the postcode, which is made up of a number and two letters, breaks down the district even further into sectors and pinpoints a street, part of a street or even a single address. Every home and business has a postcode, including Buckingham Palace.

| TN | 9 | 1 | AB |
|------|----------|--------|----------------|
| Area | District | Sector | Delivery point |

All postcoded mail travels far faster than letters with no postcode which have to be sorted by hand. So next time you write a letter, remember to quote your postcode as part of your address. Then, when people reply, they will include *your* code on the envelope.

If you are not sure of your postcode, look it up in a **Thomson's Local Directory** or check it out at a large post office or library by looking in the blue **Postcode Directory**. All London telephone directories now include postcodes and the rest of the country will follow as new directories replace the old.

This is how you should write an address on an envelope:

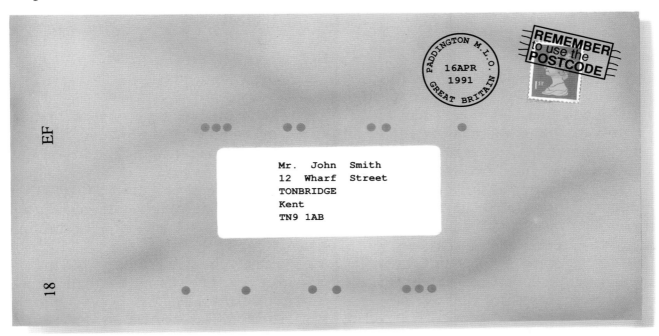

*Always write the town in block capitals and leave a clear space between the two parts of the postcode.*

The address should be written on the lower part of the envelope to make sure that the cancellation stamp does not hide part of the address.

(To learn about the blue phosphor dots on the envelope above, turn to page 23.)

*BRITAIN WAS THE FIRST COUNTRY IN THE WORLD TO INTRODUCE NUMBERED POSTAL DISTRICTS, BUT GERMANY WAS THE FIRST TO ADOPT POSTCODES.*

# Now you see

**1** *The postcode for the Prime Minister's residence at 10 Downing Street is SW1A 2AA. Find out the postcode of other famous places and also of your doctor's surgery, the library and your school.*

**2** *Failure to use the postcode causes problems. If someone writes the town but not the county, the Post Office has to make a guess as to where to send the letter, for example, Richmond – Surrey or Yorkshire? Ashford – Kent or Middlesex?*

*Find out examples of other towns with 'twins'.*

**3** *Postcodes provide a means of identifying personal property that might be stolen. Use a special marker pen to put your postcode on your bicycle or any other items you value. The ink in this kind of pen can only be seen under ultra-violet light and the identification marks can help the police to return stolen items to their owners.*

# Sorting the mail

*If you think that it costs a lot to send a letter, then just stop and think of all the processes it goes through before reaching its destination.*

A Mechanised Letter Office, called an **MLO** is a very busy and noisy place, especially during the night and early morning when first-class letters and small packets are being sorted, coded and sorted again before continuing on their journey, and finally dropping through your letter box.

Each mail bag is emptied onto a **Face Canceller Table**, where postmen sort the mail into first and second-class letters of Post Office Preferred Size envelopes or **POPS**, as they are called.

The letters are put on to conveyor belts with the stamps all facing in the same direction so they can be automatically cancelled at the far end.

Slightly larger envelopes are sorted into first or second-class pigeon holes, then taken away and run through a small stamp cancelling machine.

Larger packages are put on to the top conveyor belt. The stamps are then cancelled by hand and the envelopes dropped into either first or second-class containers.

## Coding

Only POPS envelopes go to the coding desks. Operators sit at keyboards reading the postcode on each letter which passes horizontally from right to left in front of them. This is typed on to a keyboard and translated into machine language as two lines of blue phosphor dots.

The speed is controlled by the operators, some of whom are capable of coding up to 3,000 letters an hour. Each coding desk has a number, and this, plus the operator's initials, sometimes appear to the left of the blue phosphor dots on the envelope.

*A code operator at his keyboard.*

Letters then travel along a conveyor belt to a pre-sorter which sorts the mail into a rough breakdown of areas of the country.

Many large sorting offices also have what is called an **Optical Character Reader Machine**. Although this machine is only supposed to read machine-printed addresses, it can code some mail with handwritten addresses. It is much faster than the manual coding machine.

The **Automatic Sorting Machine** 'reads' the blue phosphor dots and sorts the letters at high speed into labelled boxes.

**Outward Bound Mail** is put into mail bags, sealed and then labelled before continuing its journey by road, rail or air.

**Local Mail** is taken to another part of the sorting office and sorted into postmen's walks.

*An Automatic Sorting Machine.*

# The travelling post office

*This is the night mail crossing the border,*
*Bringing the cheque and the postal order,*
*Letters for the rich, letters for the poor,*
*The shop at the corner and the girl next door . . .*

This is the first part of a poem written by W.H. Auden for the 1936 documentary film, *Night Mail*, about the Down Special from London to Glasgow and Aberdeen.

While most of us are asleep, two thirds of all first-class letters are loaded on to Travelling Post Offices, known as **TPOs**. They then travel at speeds of 100 mph through the night, the length and breadth of Britain.

*. . . Written on paper of every hue,*
*The pink, the violet, the white and the blue;*
*The chatty, the catty, the boring, adoring,*
*The cold and official and the heart's*
  *outpouring,*
*Clever, stupid, short and long,*
*The typed and the printed and the spelt all*
  *wrong . . .*

*Crewe station at midnight, where the men and women of the Post Office are busy working inside the TPOs.*

These TPO coaches do not have any passenger seats but are fitted out as mobile sorting offices. Postmen work throughout the night sorting the mail while the train speeds on its way.

The special trains collect and deliver mail to around 120 different stations. Crewe Station is where the largest number of TPOs meet in a single place.

The team work an eight-hour shift, five nights a week. A train travelling to Aberdeen will stop at Carlisle for the English team to exchange places with a Scottish team at around two o'clock in the morning.

In railway language, all trains travel up to London and down to all places from London.

First-class letters can be posted into the side of a TPO right up to the moment it leaves the station. Some big stations also have late posting boxes on the platforms or nearby.

*325 MILLION LETTERS ARE CARRIED BY TPOs ANNUALLY.*

*TPOs TRAVEL A TOTAL OF 5.5 MILLION MILES EVERY YEAR. THAT'S THE SAME AS TRAVELLING TO THE MOON AND BACK ELEVEN TIMES!*

## Now you see

1 If you live near a mainline station, post a first-class letter in one of the boxes there. How long does the letter take to reach its destination?

2 Read the two parts of W.J. Auden's poem out loud in time to the sound of an imaginary mail train racing through the night. It is a wonderful poem, bringing the night mail very much alive. Write your own poem that brings to life any part of the Post Office today and send it to Mount Pleasant Post Office in London for comments.

# Mail Rail

*Did you know that deep below the traffic-choked streets of London there are trains which carry no passengers and have no drivers or guards?*

It's true, and this railway is owned by the Post Office. Mail Rail, as it is called, has solved the problem of the slow-moving traffic by carrying large numbers of letters and small packages across the capital city under the ground. In fact, more than 10 million bags of mail are transported by this railway every year.

The trains are automatically controlled and travel at 35 mph through 2.743 m (9 ft) diameter tubes. The track runs for a distance of 10.5 km between Paddington and Whitechapel, and links two British Rail mainline stations and six major London sorting offices. The journey takes only 26 minutes, including the stops at all the stations, while up above that same journey would take very much longer.

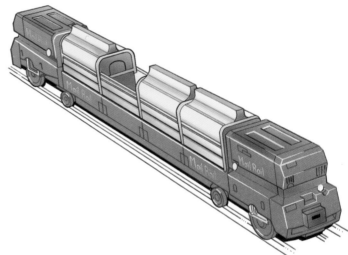

Each car has four containers and can carry fifteen bags of letters and small packages. Two cars can be joined together to take extra mail.

THERE ARE A STAGGERING 168 km OF TUNNELS USED BY LONDON UNDERGROUND TO TRANSPORT PEOPLE BENEATH THE CAPITAL CITY. THAT'S SIXTEEN TIMES MORE THAN THE LENGTH OF THE MAIL RAIL TUNNEL!

*The special battery-driven train which is used for recovering trains that break down in the Mail Rail tunnel.*

The 34 electric trains run at four-minute intervals during busy periods for 22 hours a day. Every day, the railway is shut down between 8 am and 10 am so that men can inspect the track and carry out any necessary repair work. The trains average 500 miles a week and are taken out of service for maintenance work every 8 to 10 weeks. A special green and black battery-driven train with a blue flashing light is used for recovering trains that break down in the tunnel and to tow them out of the way into a siding.

The tunnel just beyond Mount Pleasant station is surprisingly light and airy, but extremely noisy when the trains thunder through. When all is quiet, London's underground trains can be heard overhead. It is here that the tunnel runs alongside the River Fleet.

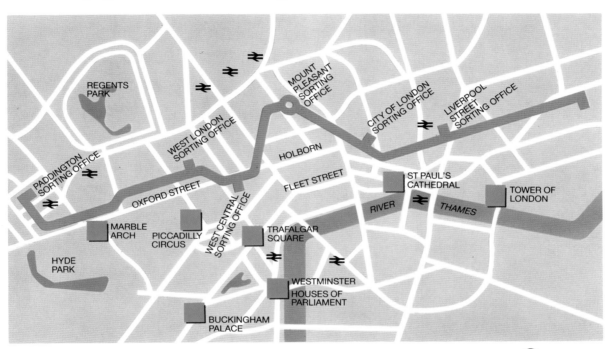

*DURING THE FIRST WORLD WAR, WHILE TUNNELLING WAS STILL IN PROGRESS, VALUABLE ART TREASURES WERE STORED IN THE TUNNELS AS A PROTECTION AGAINST BOMBING RAIDS. THEN, DURING THE SECOND WORLD WAR, THE TUNNELS WERE USED AS SHELTERS BY POST OFFICE STAFF.*

*MAIL WAS FIRST CARRIED ON THE POST OFFICE'S UNDERGROUND RAILWAY ON 3 DECEMBER 1927.*

# Now you see

*Draw your own map of the Post Office Mail Rail on a large sheet of paper. Then, with the help of a tourist map of London, search out any well-known buildings, roads and landmarks which stand above the underground railway. Find magazine pictures, postcards, drawings or photographs of these features and glue them on to your map in the correct places. Then display your collage on a wall.*

# Postage stamps

*The first adhesive postage stamp in the world was introduced in 1840. It was the Penny Black.*

### The Penny Black

The design for the world's first adhesive stamp was of the young Queen Victoria's head. (A face is very difficult to forge.) The young Queen Victoria so liked her portrait on the stamps that all stamps issued during her long reign continued to show her portrait, and the head or outline of the reigning monarch has been on our stamps ever since.

Because Britain was the first country in the world to use adhesive postage stamps, it does not have to show the country on its stamps.

At first, collectors tried to obtain as many stamps as possible from all over the world, but because the number of different stamps grew so large, this type of collection soon became impossible. It is more usual these days to concentrate on one country or a particular theme.

IN VICTORIAN TIMES, PEOPLE DECORATED ORNAMENTS, SCREENS AND EVEN THEIR WALLS WITH USED POSTAGE STAMPS.

THE FIRST PERSON OTHER THAN ROYALTY TO APPEAR ON A BRITISH STAMP WAS WILLIAM SHAKESPEARE, IN 1964.

THE FIRST SHEETS OF STAMPS HAD TO BE CUT WITH SCISSORS AS THERE WERE NO PERFORATIONS.

**Definitive Stamps** are the ordinary, 'everyday' stamps which show just the head of the reigning monarch and the value of the stamp.

**Commemorative stamps** mark special events, anniversaries and also show aspects of life in the British Isles. The design must include the value of the stamp and the monarch's head. The colours used must not weaken the glow of the phosphor which is used to help machines separate first and second-class mail. The final design has to be approved by the monarch.

**Stamp books** to the value of £1 and 50p change slightly in design around the time the commemorative stamps are issued.

**Prestige stamp books** are issued once a year. These are colourfully illustrated books on a chosen subject or anniversary containing four pages or 'panes' of nine stamps, one of which is of mixed postage values.

**First-day covers** consist of a specially-designed envelope containing the latest commemorative stamps cancelled with a pictorial first-day-of-issue postmark.

*A selection of First Day Covers (above) and Prestige Stamp Books (left).*

# Now you see

1 Find out why a special issue was chosen and something about the subject on each stamp.

2 Together with your friends, collect used stamps for a charity of your choice.

3 The Stamp Bug Club has been set up by the Post Office and has a membership of over 65,000 children worldwide. Members receive a colourful magazine, 'Stamp Bug News', six times a year, plus a calendar giving dates of special issues. If you would like to learn more about this club, write to the address given at the back of this book.

# Postcards

*On 1 October 1870, the Post Office brought out a plain postcard which was sold for the price of the ½d violet coloured stamp. One million postcards were posted in the first week. However, some people felt shy about allowing the postman to see what they had written.*

**Picture postcards** were approved by the Post Office on 1 September 1894. However, on the Continent, the craze for sending and collecting postcards had already begun. In Britain, this absorbing family hobby was slower to take off, mainly because the designs were uninteresting and the cards could only be bought in packets of six.

**Court cards** was the name given to the early British postcards. They were smaller (115 × 89 mm) than those used on the Continent (140 × 89 mm). The message had to be written on the same side as the picture, leaving the back for the stamp and the address.

In 1899, the Post Office allowed printers to change to the larger size, and two years later Britain became the first country to issue picture postcards with a divided back so that the message could be written on the left and the address on the right.

Between 1900 and 1914, the great craze began in Britain for sending and collecting postcards. Postcard publishers competed with each other to produce a wide variety of designs, and families saved the postcards they received and mounted them in albums.

After the First World War, interest in collecting postcards died out and did not start up again until the early 1970s when a travelling exhibition was put on by the Victoria and Albert Museum in London.

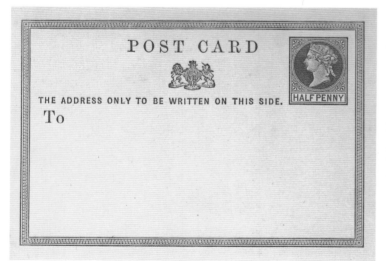

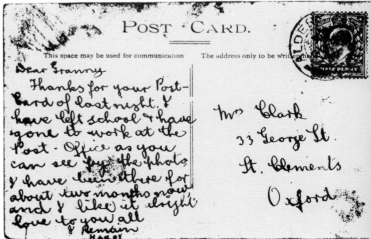

*The plain postcard introduced in 1870 (left) and a picture postcard (below) – this one sent from a Post Office worker to his grandmother.*

Loch Sheil & Prince Charlie's Monument.

A PARCEL MIS-DIRECTED HAS GONE ASTRAY SOMEHOW, I'VE RE-DIRECTED IT & HOPE IT'S ON THE RIGHT TRACK NOW.

To You

Franco-British Exhibition.

1905    Vers la Paix Universelle    1908

# Now you see

**1** A wide variety of novelty cards were produced. Picture postcard publishers, Raphael Tuck & Sons, produced picture puzzle postcards which were great favourites with the public. Try making your own jigsaw puzzle card. First, write your message on the back of a picture postcard before cutting it up into six shapes. Place the pieces into an envelope and send to a friend.

**2** Collecting postcards is fun. There are postcards on almost every subject, but take your time before deciding what to collect. One idea would be to link with one of your other interests – sport, railways or animals, for example. Once your collection is underway, use a shoe box to store your cards or put them in an album.

**3** Watch out for old postcards. Messages written on cards long ago will tell you a great deal about the people and how they lived.

# Useful addresses and places to visit

Stamp Bug Club
Freepost
PO Box 109
HIGH WYCOMBE
Bucks
HP10 8BR
*A club set up by the Post Office for young stamp collectors and anyone interested in stamps.*

Post Office Education Service
Royal Mail House
29 Wellington Street
LEEDS
L51 1DA
*Enquire about posters and booklets on the Post Office.*

The Post Office Film and Video Library
London Road Trading Estate
SITTINGBOURNE
Kent
ME10 1NQ
*Videos and films for hire or to purchase.*

The Post Office Archives
Freeling House
23 Glasshill Street
LONDON
SE1 0BQ
Tel: 071 261 1145
*Information Sheets available on the Post Office.*

The British Philatelic Bureau
20 Brandon Street
EDINBURGH
EH3 5TT
*Write for information on first-day covers, presentation packs and collectors' packs.*

The Letter Box Study Group
Mr Martin Robinson
31 Tuckwell Close
Stockton
RUGBY
Warwickshire
CV23 8JP
*If you find some interesting and unusual boxes, send the details to the above address. If you want information, don't forget to enclose a stamped addressed envelope. Useful information can be obtained in Shire Book No.188 called* Old Letter Boxes *by Martin Robinson, ISBN 0 85263 846 9.*

The Scout and Guide Stamp Club
Mr Peter Duck
256 St Margarets Road
TWICKENHAM
Middlesex
TW11 PR
*A stamp club for both adults and young people in the Scout and Guide Movements.*

Postal Mechanisation Study Circle
J.H.F. Notton
16 Crawshay Drive
Emmer Green
READING
RG4 8SX
*The main aim of the above is the recording and archiving of information about the mechanisation process of the Post Office.*

## Places to visit

National Postal Museum
King Edward Street
LONDON
EC14 1LP
Tel: 071 239 5420
*Open Mon-Thurs. 10–4.30 pm*
*           Fri.      10–4 pm*
*Closed Saturday, Sunday and Bank Holidays*
*Admission free*

Bath Postal Museum
8 Broad Street
BATH
BA1 5LJ
Tel: 0225 60333
*Videos on the Post Office are shown regularly.*
*Ring for details.*

The National Railway Museum
Leeman Road
YORK
YO2 4XJ
*Sometimes a TPO coach is on display.*

Post Office Underground Railway
Room 231
148-166 Old Street
LONDON
EC1V 9HQ
Tel: 071 250 2141
*Visits can be arranged to include Mount Pleasant Sorting Office. There are also special open days in October for young people and their families. Write or telephone for further information.*

Didcot Railway Centre
Tel: 0235 817200
*Ring for details of their demonstrations of a mail drop.*

**Acknowledgements**
The author and publishers would like to thank the following for their invaluable help with this book:
Mr Moss Foley, National Schools Officer; Mr Martin Robinson, author of *Rare British Letter Boxes*; Mr Alex Obradovich (TPOs); Mr Harry Reeves, the National Postal Museum; Mr Derek Varrier Mail Rail, Mount Pleasant; Mr Paul Mills, trainer at Tonbridge Sorting Office; Mr Philip Moore, Royal Mail Stamps and Philately; Mr David Redpath, Postman; Mr Pat Donachie and Mr Jon Weller, Postal Cadet Trainers; Mr Barry Wiles, Post Office Video Library; Mr J. H. F. Notton of the Postal Mechanisation Study Circle; The Post Office Archives; Mr Peter Howe, the Post Office Photographic Library. The publishers would also like to thank the following for permission to reproduce photographic material in the book:
The National Postal Museum p.13, p.31; Royal Mail Stamps p.6; Chris Watts p.25; all other photographic material: The Post Office Photographic Library.

**British Library Cataloguing-in-Publication Data**
Barrow, Jean
  The post office project book. – (project books)
  I. Title   II. Series 383

ISBN 0-340-55840-7

First published 1992

© 1992 Jean Barrow

Typeset by Litho Link Ltd, Welshpool, Powys.
Printed in Hong Kong for the educational publishing division of Hodder and Stoughton Ltd, Mill Road, Dunton Green, Sevenoaks, Kent by Colorcraft.